PIANO/VOCAL/CHORDS

POPULAR SHEET MUSIC HITS

Published 2004

© International Music Publications Ltd
Griffin House, 14 Hammersmith Road London W6 8BS England

Editorial management by (www.artemismusic.com)
Reproducing is illegal and forbidden by the
Copyrights Act, 1988

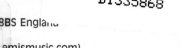

All I Wanna Do

Words and Music by Sheryl Crow, Wyn Cooper, Kevin Gilbert, William Bottrell and David Baerwald

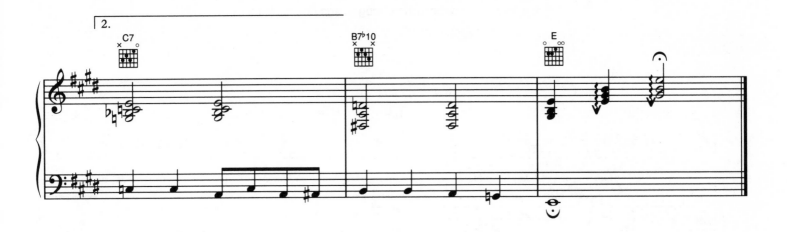

Verse 3:
I like a good beer buzz early in the morning
And Billy likes to peel the labels from his bottles of Bud
And shred them on the bar
Then he lights every match in an oversized pack
Letting each one burn down to his thick fingers
Before blowing and cursing them out
And he's watching the Buds as they spin on the floor
A happy couple enters the bar, dancing dangerously close to one another
The bartender looks up from his want ads

Amazing

Words and Music by Jonathan Douglas and George Michael

Because You Loved Me

Words and Music by Diane Warren

18

As Time Goes By

Words and Music by Herman Hupfeld

must get down to earth, at times re- lax, re- lieve the ten- sion. No

mat- ter what the prog- ress, or what may yet be proved, The

sim- ple facts of life are such they can- not be re- moved. You

must re- mem- ber this, a kiss is still a kiss, a sigh is just a sigh;

Complicated

Words and Music by Avril Lavigne, Lauren Christy, David Alspach and Graham Edwards

Foolish Games

Words and Music by Jewel Kilcher

* Vocal sung one octave lower

Verse 2:
You're always the mysterious one with
Dark eyes and careless hair,
You were fashionably sensitive
But too cool to care.
You stood in my doorway with nothing to say
Besides some comment on the weather.
(To Pre-Chorus:)

Verse 3:
You're always brilliant in the morning,
Smoking your cigarettes and talking over coffee.
Your philosophies on art, Baroque moved you.
You loved Mozart and you'd speak of your loved ones
As I clumsily strummed my guitar.

Verse 4:
You'd teach me of honest things,
Things that were daring, things that were clean.
Things that knew what an honest dollar did mean.
I hid my soiled hands behind my back.
Somewhere along the line, I must have gone
Off track with you.

Pre-Chorus 2:
Excuse me, think I've mistaken you for somebody else,
Somebody who gave a damn, somebody more like myself.
(To Chorus:)

I Turn To You

Words and Music by Diane Warren

1. When the world is dark - er than I can un - der - stand,_____
(Verse 2 see block lyrics)

if you've lost your way, you could turn to me

like I turn to you.

D.%. al Coda

I turn to you

Verse 2:
When my insides are wracked with anxiety
You have the touch that will quiet me
You lift my spirit, you melt the ice
When I need inspiration, when I need advice.

I turn to you *etc.*

The Greatest Love Of All

Words by Linda Creed
Music by Michael Masser

Chorus:

I Could Not Ask For More

Words and Music by Diane Warren

I Will Always Love You

Words and Music by Dolly Parton

There You'll Be

Words and Music by Diane Warren

Lean On Me

Words and Music by Bill Withers

My Way

Music by Jacques Revaux and Claude Francois
Words by Gilles Thibaut
Translation by Paul Anka

Now And Forever

Words and Music by Richard Marx

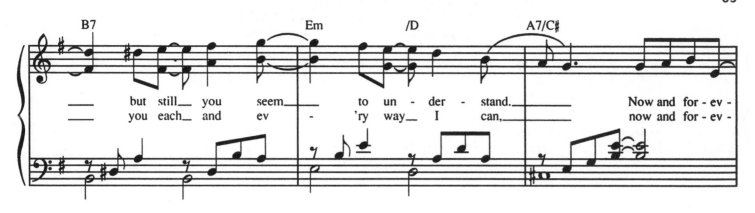

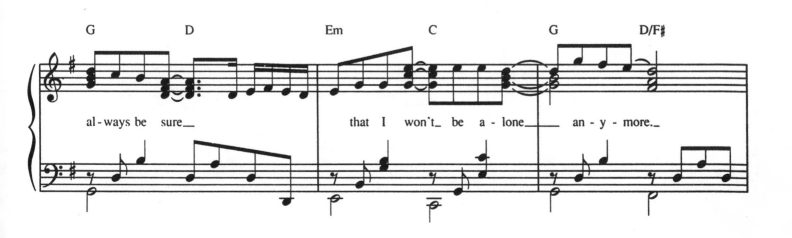

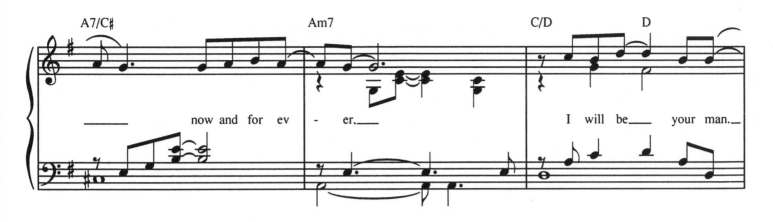

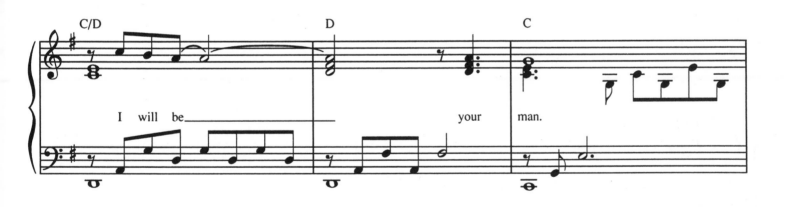

Obvious

Words and Music by Andreas Carlsson, Carl Falk, Carl Bjorssel, Sebastian Thott, Didrik Thott and Savan Kotecha

Over The Rainbow

Words by E Y Harburg
Music by Harold Arlen

When all the world is a hope-less jum-ble and the rain-drops tum-ble all a-round,

heav - en o-pens a mag-ic lane.

When all the clouds dark-en up the sky-way, there's a rain - bow high-way to be found,

The Prayer

Words and Music by Carole Bayer-Sager and David Foster

The Rose

Words and Music by Amanda McBroom

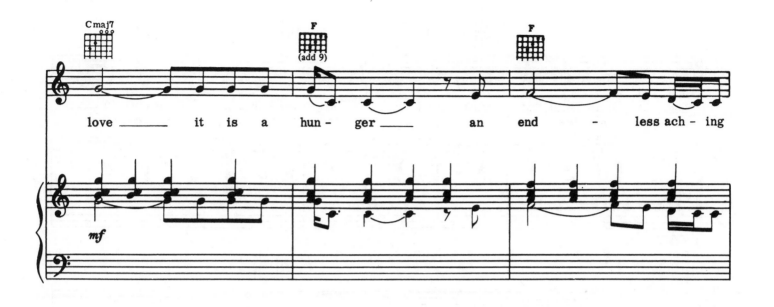

love ____ it is a hun - ger ____ an end - less ach - ing

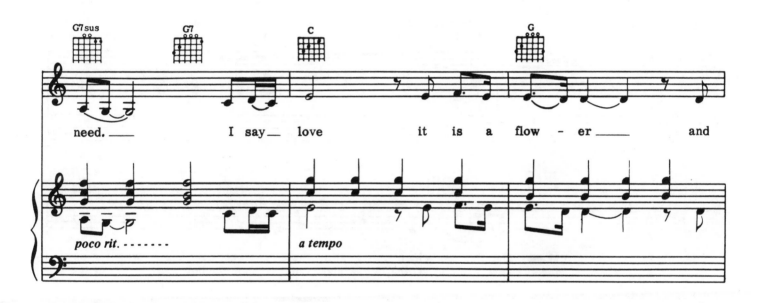

need. ____ I say ___ love it is a flow - er ____ and

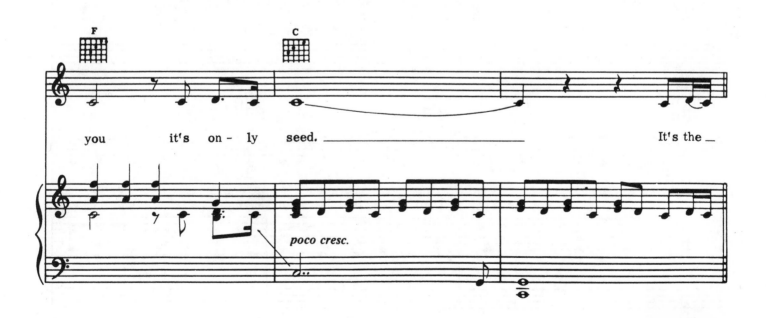

you it's on - ly seed. _____ It's the _

Something About The Way
You Look Tonight

Words by Bernie Taupin
Music by Elton John

Theme from *New York, New York*

Words by Fred Ebb
Music by John Kander

To Where You Are

Words and Music by Richard Marx and Linda Thompson

Unbreak My Heart

Words and Music by Diane Warren

Come back__ and say__ you love__ me.   Un - break__ my   heart,__ sweet dar - ling.

With - out__ you, I__ just can't__ go_____ on._____

Repeat ad lib. and fade

The Wind Beneath My Wings

Words and Music by Larry Henley and Jeff Silbar

Vogue

Words and Music by Madonna Ciccone and Shep Pettibone

Spoken: What are you looking at?   Vogue!   Strike a pose . . . . Vogue!

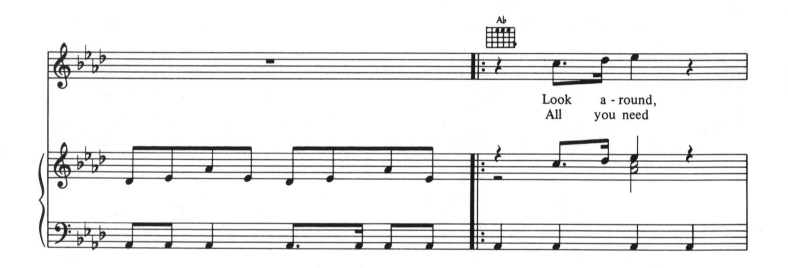

Look a - round,
All you need

ev - 'ry-where you turn is heart - ache, it's ev - 'ry-where that you go.
is your own i - ma - gi - na - tion so use it, that's what it's for.

D.%. al Coda ⊕ *CODA* x4 Ab no3

get up on the dance__ floor.__

(Here is where you find it!)

Ab Fb Ebm Fb

Vogue!

Greta Garbo, and Monroe, Dietrich and Di Maggio,
They had style, they had grace, Rita Hayward gave good face

Tacet 1°

Ab Fb Ebm Fb Ab Fb

Marlon Brando, Jimmy Dean on the cover of a magazine. Grace Kelly, Harlow Jean,
Lauren, Katherine, Lana too, Betty Davis, we loved you, ladies with an attitude

Ebm Fb Ab Fb Ebm Fb

picture of a beauty queen. Gene Kelly, Fred Astaire, Ginger Rogers, dance on air.
fellas that were In The Mood. Don't just stand there, let's get to it, strike a pose, there's nothing to it.

Smash!

Alphabetical Songfinder

YOU'RE THE VOICE

8861A PV/CD

Casta Diva from Norma – Vissi D'arte from Tosca – Un Bel Di Vedremo from Madama Butterfly – Addio, Del Passato from La Traviata – J'ai Perdu Mon Eurydice from Orphee Et Eurydice – Les Tringles Des Sistres Tintaient from Carmen – Porgi Amor from Le Nozze Di Figaro – Ave Maria from Otello

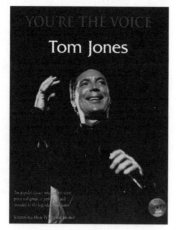

8860A PVG/CD

Delilah – Green Green Grass Of Home – Help Yourself – I'll Never Fall In Love Again – It's Not Unusual – Mama Told Me Not To Come – Sexbomb – Thunderball – What's New Pussycat – You Can Leave Your Hat On

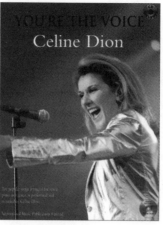

9297A PVG/CD

Beauty And The Beast – Because You Loved Me – Falling Into You – The First Time Ever I Saw Your Face – It's All Coming Back To Me Now – Misled – My Heart Will Go On – The Power Of Love – Think Twice – When I Fall In Love

9349A PVG/CD

Chain Of Fools – A Deeper Love Do Right Woman, Do Right Man – I Knew You Were Waiting (For Me) – I Never Loved A Man (The Way I Loved You) – I Say A Little Prayer – Respect – Think – Who's Zooming Who – (You Make Me Feel Like) A Natural Woman

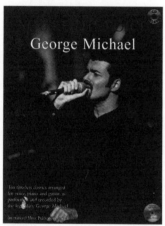

9007A PVG/CD

Careless Whisper – A Different Corner – Faith – Father Figure – Freedom '90 – I'm Your Man – I Knew You Were Waiting (For Me) – Jesus To A Child – Older – Outside

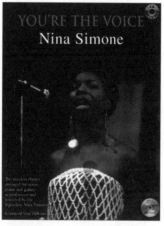

9606A PVG/CD

Don't Let Me Be Misunderstood – Feeling Good – I Loves You Porgy – I Put A Spell On You – Love Me Or Leave Me – Mood Indigo – My Baby Just Cares For Me – Ne Me Quitte Pas (If You Go Away) – Nobody Knows You When You're Down And Out – Take Me To The Water

9700A PVG/CD

Beautiful – Crying In The Rain – I Feel The Earth Move – It's Too Late – (You Make Me Feel Like) A Natural Woman – So Far Away – Way Over Yonder – Where You Lead – Will You Love Me Tomorrow – You've Got A Friend

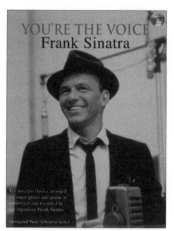

9746A PVG/CD

April In Paris – Come Rain Or Come Shine – Fly Me To The Moon (In Other Words) – I've Got You Under My Skin – The Lady Is A Tramp – My Kinda Town (Chicago Is) – My Way – Theme From New York, New York – Someone To Watch Over Me – Something Stupid

9770A PVG/CD

Cry Me A River – Evergreen (A Star Is Born) – Happy Days Are Here Again – I've Dreamed Of You – Memory – My Heart Belongs To Me – On A Clear Day (You Can See Forever) – Someday My Prince Will Come – Tell Him (duet with Celine Dion) – The Way We Were

9799A PVG/CD

Boogie Woogie Bugle Boy – Chapel Of Love – Friends – From A Distance – Hello In There – One For My Baby (And One More For The Road) – Only In Miami – The Rose – When A Man Loves A Woman – Wind Beneath My Wings

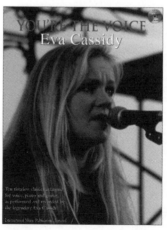

9810A PVG/CD

Ain't No Sunshine – Autumn Leaves – How Can I Keep From Singing – Imagine – It Doesn't Matter Anymore – Over The Rainbow – Penny To My Name – People Get Ready – Wayfaring Stranger – What A Wonderful World

9889A PVG/CD

Around The World – Born Free – From Russia With Love – Gonna Build A Mountain – The Impossible Dream – My Kind Of Girl – On A Clear Day You Can See Forever – Portrait Of My Love – Softly As I Leave You – Walk Away

The outstanding vocal series from IMP

CD contains full backings for each song, professionally arranged to recreate the sounds of the original recording